BUTTERFLY WISDOM™

Four Passages to Transformation

By Joyce C. Mills, Ph.D.

ISBN 9780967328010

Published by Imaginal Press:
10249 N. 25th Street Phoenix, AZ 85028
www.drjoycemills.com
adapted from Reconnecting to the Magic of Life.

*W*ings Happen when you Hear the music,
Dance with zest, Laugh out loud, Taste passion,
See the rainbows, Feel your wings and Soar.

Table of Contents

When you know where you are,
you'll know where you're going.

PART I
The Story

Universally viewed as a symbol of transformation and healing, butterflies entrance, delight, and embrace the hearts of those who seek an understanding of personal growth and change. A story comes to mind here as told to me by a traditional Storyteller from the Warm Springs Tribe. I share it with you in the way that I remember it.

...And so it is said a long, long time ago there were two Caterpillar People who were very much in love. One day a sad thing happened and the Caterpillar Man died. The heart of the Caterpillar Woman was broken. She didn't want to see anyone or talk to anyone and so she wrapped her sorrow around her like a shawl. Then she began walking and walking...and while she walked, she cried.

Caterpillar woman walked for a whole year, and because the earth is a circle, she returned to the very place from which she had begun walking. The Creator took great pity on her, saying, "You have suffered too long. Now it is the time to step into a new world of color...a new world of great beauty." Then the Creator clapped hands twice...and the Woman burst forth from the shawl as a beautiful butterfly. And it is told that this is why the butterfly is a symbol of renewal for many communities...it tells us that at the end of all suffering, there is the gift of relief.

Spiritually, this ancient story provides us with an important teaching about healing, change, and renewal. Scientifically, there is also another story which can help us to see how each stage of the butterfly's transformation parallels our own stages of change.

One spring day back in 1987, a very dear friend of mine, Diana Linden, a neurophysiological biologist at Occidental College, and I were discussing the use of metaphors to explain science. Diana enjoyed using stories to teach biology to her classes and I enjoyed listening to her talk about her amazing research into muscular dystrophy. During this visit, she asked me how I viewed healing. Pondering my response for a moment, an image of a butterfly came to mind. "When I think of healing, I think about the butterfly. You know, we are like a caterpillar crawling around, until at one point or another, we go inside our cocoon and transform into a butterfly." Chuckling a bit, Diana said, "Oh, Joyce, that's not exactly what happens. You're leaving out a big part of the process of transformation." She went on to tell me the story.

"As most of us know, there are four stages to the butterfly's transformation... the Egg, the Caterpillar, the Chrysalis, and the Emerging Butterfly. What most of us don't know is what makes the metamorphosis possible...what changes the caterpillar into a butterfly. Caterpillars have special cells in their bodies called "imaginal discs," which contain all the seeds of change."

Imaginal discs, I echoed within myself. Even though I really didn't know what they were, I knew that I could certainly use something magical to help me release my personal seeds of change whenever I felt stuck in one place or another in my life. "Where can I get some?" I humorously quipped. Diana laughed along with me and then continued...

"You see, the caterpillar prepares for this great change by eating and eating. When it is big enough, it shakes its body and sheds its skin, which it has now outgrown...shakes and sheds, shakes and sheds. Then just at the right time, it finds a leaf or a branch and attaches itself by weaving

a thin silkened thread and a small pad, becoming what is known as the chrysalis. The chrysalis is a hardened skin that develops and protects the caterpillar as it goes through its changes. Inside of the chrysalis the caterpillar completely breaks down in structure, becoming a soupy-like substance.

It is only at the point of this breakdown that the imaginal discs release the seeds of change contained within, allowing the caterpillar to transform itself into a beautiful butterfly. Even after it's fully formed, the butterfly needs all of its own strength to push itself through the constraints of the chrysalis. Once out, its wings are still wet and needs time before it is ready to fly. If hurried, it will be crippled for life. And so the magic of metamorphosis completes itself.

As this model of transformational change and healing began to unfold, I realized that so often in life we all go through the greatest times of uncertainty, fear, darkness, feeling like "I can't take one more thing." Then somehow after what could be called a "moment of miracle," we find the inner strength...our own imaginal discs... to go on and eventually experience a breakthrough in our personal, business, and spiritual growth.

Seasons of Transformation

The cycles of the seasons also parallel the butterfly's four stages of change and our own passages to personal and professional growth. In the *Summer* there is often intense heat. This season is similar to the mature passion igniting a mating dance, whereby the butterfly finds a safe leaf on which to lay eggs to support the next stage of development.

That intense heat evolves into *Fall*, when the leaves change from green to vibrant colors, only to become brittle and then fall off the trees. This season is likened to the Caterpillar stage of the butterfly, when this little furry creature sheds its outer skin several times, while preparing for the next stage of its transformative development. Then there is *Winter*, often appearing cold, barren with an absence of color and vibrancy. In essence, all is asleep, dormant, or hibernating. The season of *Winter* is most like this Chrysalis stage – all the changes are taking place on an inner level.

Staying with quiet space and a time of not-knowing – not having clear-cut answers or quick solutions to our problems – withdrawal from the outside world – is not often honored in our society. We are supposed to have the answers and be able to come up with solutions at the drop of a hat. Yet, nature tells us that this is a critical time in the life cycle of change. It is important to remember that all creatures of nature have a time of withdrawal, dormancy, or hibernation. There is a life-cycle pattern that allows for a time of cocooning.

Likewise, beneath the chrysalis of the earth, within the womb of her caves, life is preparing to regenerate. This regeneration reveals itself during the next season, *Spring*. It is a reawakening of life – playful, youthful, and colorful. The four stages of the butterfly are very much like the four seasons of nature. There must be the season of Chrysalis before the season of Emerging Butterfly.

PART II
The Four Passages Of Transformation

Journey with me as we take a closer look at how each of the four stages of the butterfly and the four seasons parallel the passages we experience in our quest for personal growth, change, and healing.

THE FIRST PASSAGE: THE EGG STAGE

Summer

Intense heat, mature passion, and mating mark this season.

THE SECOND PASSAGE: THE CATERPILLAR STAGE

Fall

When the leaves transform from green to vibrant colors, only to become brittle and then fall off of the trees readying for the next passage of change.

THE THIRD PASSAGE: THE CHRYSALIS STAGE

Winter

Withdrawal, dormancy, or hibernation, all is asleep. All the changes are taking place on an inner level.

THE FOURTH PASSAGE: EMERGING BUTTERFLY STAGE

Spring

Regeneration reveals itself during this season. It is a reawakening of life, of nature. It is a time of emergence. Spring is playful, youthfully passionate, and fluttering.

Summer

Intense heat, mature passion,
and mating mark this season.

New Beginnings

In the world of the butterfly, I learned that after a time of an elaborate courtship dance with the sole or "soul" purpose of attracting the opposite sex and mating, the female selects just the right plant on which to lay her eggs. She does this so that her eggs have a safe home on which to hatch. Paralleling this first stage we find the importance of connecting with our passion, from which the mating of ideas is birthed. It is essential to create a safe environment in which all new ideas, relationships, and personal awarenesses have the opportunity of developing. Without this safe environment, nothing positive develops. We need support to go on.

Think back to the moment when you had a new idea that you were so passionate about and went to share it with someone.

- How did that person respond?
- What was he or she doing when you were talking?
- Was he looking around or was she glancing at her watch at the time?
- Did you get the message to go on, or forget it?

Take stock. If someone new is coming into your business, how do you welcome him or her? Was there a note, flowers, an invitation to lunch… or was the person just shown to his or her office and told "If you need something, call?" Is your environment – whether it be home or business – one that nurtures an inner well-spring of creative passion? In order to encourage positive change, healing, and empowerment, it is essential to provide a supportive "leaf" on which people feel safe to lay the eggs of their ideas. This stage protects and incubates that which is new.

Fall

When the leaves transform from green to
vibrant colors, only to become brittle and then fall off of the
trees *readying* for the next passage of change.

Preparing For Change

Have you ever said to yourself any of the following statements? "I am not happy in this relationship? I am outgrowing my partner, job, or lifestyle." "I know that I need to make some changes in my life." "I need to shed my skin and become a new person," "I'm not happy living in this body." Well, if you have pondered any of these thoughts, it is a good indicator that you have entered the *second passage* of transformation.

Like the caterpillar, we know it is time for a change in our lives. We may express feelings of being bored with life, of wanting to move on in some way. Sometimes people may gain a great deal of weight during this stage, saying they feel like eating everything in sight I remember a good friend of mine in Los Angeles telling me that in Yoga teachings they say that just before a great change in life, one gains a great deal of weight. Then when the change completes itself, the weight seems to fall away.

Oftentimes, there just seems to be an overall sense of discontentment with life as it is in this second passage, but discontentment is not necessarily always negative It is can be used as a positive indicator pointing to the need for change in our lives or letting us know that change is on the way whether we have asked for it or not.

Think of the Fall season when people flock to the New England states to see the leaves changing colors. It is nature's palette letting us know that change is on the way. Becoming brittle, the leaves fall off of the trees leaving them bare, naked, without outer beauty. Like the instar stage of the caterpillar when it sheds its skin several times in preparation for its next passage of development, Fall is *readying* itself for the next season of change.

Winter

Withdrawal, dormancy, or hibernation, all is asleep.
All the changes are taking place on an inner level.

Dark Spaces Of Change

This third passage creates the greatest attention as to the mystery of change. With the chrysalis completely formed, the caterpillar is now ready to "break down" and have its special cells, the imaginal discs, release the seeds of change. While the chrysalis appearing inactive, quiet on the outside, the most amazing and dramatic changes take place on the inside. *It is during this stage that the magic of transformation takes place.* Like the butterfly, it is in this stage that our greatest change occurs as well.

Our chrysalis stage is often marked as a peak time of "not knowing." It is a period of withdrawal, not wanting to socialize, often wanting to hide and not deal with the outside world, with a given struggle, or with a certain situation. I often hear clients say, "I just want to pull the covers over my head and not face anyone...I want to wake up and have this problem gone...I can't see a way out of this situation... my life feels hopeless." Life often feels dark and isolated with little space for outer movement. Although some people view these feelings as symptoms of depression or anxiety, I choose to view these same symptoms as indicators of being in this third stage...the chrysalis...the place where the greatest change can occur.

Like the caterpillar which must break down into a soupy, gel-like substance before releasing its seeds of change, so too do we need to learn how to break down old limiting belief systems about ourselves in order to transform from our caterpillar-like selves into empowered human beings capable of reaching our full-winged potential.

Perhaps you will be able to see that this dark space of change is truly *life's gift wrapping.* Once opened, I hope you will discover a new *present* waiting.

Spring

Regeneration reveals itself during this season.
It is a reawakening of life, of nature. It is a time of emergence.
Spring is playful, youthfully passionate, and fluttering.

Wings Happen

A long time ago I heard a story about a man who found a large cocoon and decided to take it home to watch the butterfly inside emerge. As I remember it, the man watched and watched until one day he noticed a tiny opening in the cocoon. He thought the butterfly was struggling to make its way out of the cocoon and that something must be wrong. So he decided to help the butterfly along by making a larger slit for it to emerge with greater ease. When the butterfly finally came out, its wings were somewhat shriveled and small and its body misshapen. The man thought that the wings would spread out in a few hours, but they did not. Instead the butterfly was unable to fly...it was crippled for life. Although the man was well meaning, he did not know that there was a purpose for the struggle; it was nature's way of propelling the body's fluid into the wings of the butterfly so that it could emerge and ultimately fly with strength and beauty.

This story shows us that even though the butterfly is completely formed, it has to use all of its pulsating strength to push itself through its protective chrysalis into the light. It then hangs upside-down, gently fluttering its still-wet wings. You see, even though the butterfly is fully developed and born into the world, it is not quite ready for flight. If the wet-winged butterfly is rushed along, it will be crippled for life. The butterfly knows when it is time to fly...no one has to tell it or coax it.

In our own lives, the beginning of this fourth passage is often marked by our taking more and more risks...flexing our newly acquired wings, so to speak. On an inner level we experience the first inklings of hopefulness after a dark time of unconscious change. This passage is a time of awakenings... of "ah-ha" insights...of breaking through our cocoon. It is critical to our well-being that we not be pushed during this stage, but supported to move forward at our own pace. Just as the butterfly awaits the right time to fly, at a certain point we will feel ready to assert ourselves in the world.

We begin to feel more secure with our new learnings and abilities. We may take that leap of faith to change jobs, enroll in a class we have thought about for some time, initiate a new friendship or relationship, or take that long-envisioned trip. Whatever outer action is chosen, we are ready to fly with new wings of vision and courage.

Recognizing My Wings

How do we know when we are in this fourth passage? Review the following sentences and see if they sound familiar. "I feel like I'm finally beginning to see the light at the end of the tunnel." "I feel like I could soar." "I can finally hear the music in my life again." "These ideas are finally taking off." If you have experienced any of these feelings, you will know that you are well into the fourth passage of change.

Whether we are creatively involved in a project, exploring new relationships, or encountering life's challenges, we can see the four passages leading to the miracle of change in all that we do…if we just take the time to look. Sometimes we look, but do not see. We listen, but do not hear. We touch, but do not feel. For me the butterfly speaks the language of healing and determination. She flutters by and invites our attention to her silent magic…her ability to crawl, to withdraw, to break down, to reform, to break through, and to soar.

PART III
Imaginal Discs

Seeds Of Change

At this point you may be asking, "So what's the magic that's going to transform me from a caterpillar to a butterfly?" The answer is *Imaginal Discs*. Yes, like the butterfly each of us also have imaginal discs that contain all "seeds of change." These imaginal discs are our inner resources, interests, skills, and past learnings–just lying dormant and, in a sense, just waiting to be awakened...to be released. Just as the little caterpillar carries these cells within its fuzzy body, we too carry these cells within our caterpillar stage selves...not knowing, consciously, that we even have them or what they can do for us when their "time" comes. I like to think of imaginal discs as our "winged assets" of change, enabling us to renew a sense of hope, recognizing that unseen possibilities are truly present to help us move forward, no matter what challenge or obstacle is placed in our paths.

When we look at a little caterpillar, do we ever see these magical cells? No, not consciously. But they <u>are</u> there. These cells of change contain and protect all of the mystery that transforms the caterpillar into the butterfly.

Take a few moments to reflect on those things you enjoy doing in your life, be they hobbies, interests, or things that are simply delight-ful to do, such as watching a sunset, the first snow of the season, birds singing, or your favorite flowers.

By identifying our own *imaginal discs* we are better equipped to con-front our greatest struggles and fears with a certain confidence. This is confidence that allows us to overcome self-doubt, fear, and pain so that we may reach a rich Soul life filled with joy and empowerment.

PART IV
Butterfly Wisdom Cards

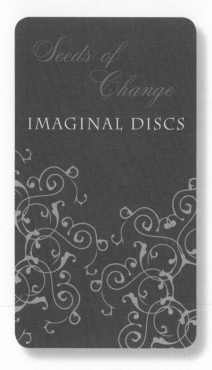

Guidelines for Using the Butterfly Wisdom Spreads

When you know where you are, you'll know where you're going.
Whether it be in your personal life or business, it is important to recognize where you are in the process and what you can do to facilitate your journey.

The following four-card spreads are offered to you as guides in your quest for transformation, change, and healing. A suggestion is to look beyond the literal meaning of the words and messages written on the cards, as each spread tells a deeper story. Notice how each word and message relates to the others you have chosen. There is a theme that always connects them.

As you become more familiar with using the cards in the decks, feel free to create your own spreads as they unfold in your consciousness.

The 32 Butterfly Wisdom action cards are designed to support you on your journey of transformational change. These cards are divided into two decks: 20 cards in the "Passages deck" and 12 cards in the "Imaginal Disc" deck.

PASSAGES DECK

The 20 cards in this deck are divided into four passages of transformation; Egg, Caterpillar, Chrysalis, Emerging Butterfly There are five cards for each of the four passages with one guidance word, the corresponding season, and a message written on each card. The Passage cards are designed to help you see where you are in your quest for change and provide guidance for your journey.

IMAGINAL DISCS DECK

The 12 Imaginal Disc cards focus on recognizing what I like to call our "Winged Assets" of change, enabling us to renew a sense of hope, recognizing that unseen possibilities are truly present to help us move forward, no matter what challenge or obstacle is placed in our paths. These Winged Assets are things you like to do and experiences that delight your senses. They bring joy to your heart, enhance creativity, and a smile to your lips.

The messages on each card will remind you of your inner resources, strengths, personal gifts, and skills while going through each passage.

Meditation for Beginning Your Journey

Before any spread, take a few moments to quiet your mind and center yourself. Begin by closing your eyes and taking a few slow deep breaths inhaling through your nose and exhaling through your mouth just like you are blowing on a soft feather. After a few breaths, open your eyes and let your intuition choose whichever spread is right for you at this time.

1. INNER BALANCE SPREAD

All of us have times in our lives when we feel overwhelmed with decisions and demands. Use this two-card spread as a way of bringing balance into your busy, everyday life.

Shuffle each deck separately and place each of them face down in front of you in two piles.

Begin by meditating on a question that relates to your personal life or business. The more open ended the question, the more information you will garner. For example, (1) "What do I need to know right now that will be most helpful to me in my personal life?" (2) With all of the decisions I need to make, what do I most need to know right now to help me feel balanced? Avoid questions that require a "yes" or "no" answer.

Choose one card from the Passages deck and one card from the Imaginal Disc deck. Read the guidance word and message on both cards. Focus on how each word and message relates to your question and your life. The word, season and message on the Passages card tells you where you are in relation to your question. The word and message on the Imaginal Disc card are the balancing seeds within your process of change.

2. INTUITION SPREAD

This spread is designed to help you develop and fine tune your personal instincts and insights as you journey through each of the four passages.

Turn each of the 20 cards in the Passages deck face up and arrange them in its rightful passage. There will be five cards in each passage. Next, turn each of the 12 cards in the Imaginal Disc deck face up as well.

Clear your mind and center your body. Next, focus on a question that relates to your personal or business life. Be clear with your question. For example, "What would be most helpful for me to know as I pursue the new career I have been thinking about?"

Look at the five cards in each passage and let your *intuition* choose one card from each of the four passages. You will have a total of four cards placed face up in front of you.

1ST PASSAGE CARD: This card represents what you will need to know as you begin your journey.

2ND PASSAGE CARD: This card indicates the signals related to your preparation for change.

3RD PASSAGE CARD: This card centers on illuminating the lessons associated with being in the dark spaces of uncertainty.

4TH PASSAGE CARD: Illuminates the message that Wings Happen.

Next choose four cards from the Imaginal Disc deck and intuitively place them face up next to the cards you have chosen from each passage. Each of these cards activate your inner resources and soulful gifts that supports each passage of your journey.

Meditate on the word, season, and message on each card. You have now intuitively chosen your course that will guide you through each passage.

3. TRANSFORMATION SPREAD

This spread focuses on transforming your *intentions* from idea to realization.

Shuffle each deck separately and place them face down before you. Take a few moments once again to clear your mind and center yourself with the breathing exercise previously mentioned. Meditate on an intention you may have been contemplating and let it surface to your consciousness. For example, your *intention* may be to start a new business or to improve a personal relationship.

With the cards still face down, randomly choose four cards from the Passages deck and one card from the Imaginal Disc deck. The cards you choose from the Passages deck represent the wings and the card you choose from the Imaginal Disc deck represents the body of the butterfly.

Place the four Passage cards in a row. Next place the Imaginal Disc card in the center. There will be two Passages cards to the left and two Passage cards to the right of the Imaginal Disc card.

IMAGINAL DISC CARD – This card provides the essence your heart needs to stay connected to as your *intention* develops its wings.

The Guidance words, seasons, and messages on each of the PASSAGES CARDS illuminate the wisdom teachings that will become the wings.

Turn the center (Imaginal Disc) card over first. The word and message on this card will be the heart to your *intention*. It will provide the resource you will need to stay connected to as your wings develop.

Next turn each of the four Passages cards over one at a time, starting from either side of the center Imaginal Disc card. Notice what each word and message tells you about that particular passage and how it relates to your *intention*. Continue turning each Passages card over until all four are face up and you have read them all.

You may find that you have randomly chosen four cards from the same passage. This will let you know that this is the passage your *intention* is in right now.

4. IMAGINAL DISC SPREAD

Life challenges can often cloud our abilities to see clearly and find positive solutions.

The purpose of this spread is to bring forward those inner resources, gifts, and skills that bring joy to your heart, a smile to your lips, and nurturing to your soul. By doing so, you are fortified with "Winged Assets" to overcome obstacles and pursue your quest for change.

Begin by shuffling the Imaginal Disc deck and placing it face down in front of you. Next, close your eyes, clear your mind and center yourself, and let a question related to overcoming obstacles float to the surface of your mind.

An example of a question could be: "What are three things I need to know right now that can help me overcome obstacles lying in my path to success?"

Choose three cards from the deck. Next, turn one card over at a time and read the word and message revealed to you on each card.

IMAGINAL DISC CARD 1 – YOUR HEART – This card represents what you need to nourish your creative passion and the heart of your ideas.

IMAGINAL DISC CARD 2 – YOUR SPIRIT – This card nourishes your spirit and the spirit of your intentions.

IMAGINAL DISC CARD 3 – YOUR MIND – This card lets you know what will help your mind stay clear and remain in the present moment.

Use these cards as affirmations to nourish your ideas in the same way you would take a drink of water to quench your thirst.

May you continue discovering
your full-winged potential as you journey forward
on your path of transformation.

Personal Reflection

Personal Reflection

Find out even more about Dr. Joyce Mills,
Her speaking engagements, consulting work, training programs,
retreats and products by visiting her website at:

www.drjoycemills.com

Acknowledgements:

To Jodi Deros, Creative Director of ATOMdesign, my heartfelt
gratitude for being in my life as the "creative dula" of my vision.
Her unmatched talent, spirit, and dedication to bringing
Butterfly Wisdom to fruition continues to nourish my soul
and inspire creativity.

To my husband Eddie, who continues to pollinate my life
with love and support. To my sons Todd and Casey, "daughter"
Lynette, and grandsons Tyler and Parker, the flowers who are forever
blooming in my garden.

And to all of the Butterflies who continue to touch my heart
in so many ways, I say Thank You.